Occupied:

Vienna is a Broken Man

&

Daughter of Hunger

Also by Kika Dorsey

Coming Up for Air
Rust
Beside Herself

Occupied:
Vienna is a Broken Man
&
Daughter of Hunger

Poems by Kika Dorsey

PINYON PUBLISHING
Montrose, Colorado

Copyright © 2020 by Kika Dorsey

All rights reserved. Except as permitted under the U.S. Copyright Act of 1976, no part of this publication may be reproduced, distributed, or transmitted in any form or by any means, or stored in a database or retrieval system, without the prior written permission of the publisher, except for brief quotations in articles, books, and reviews.

Cover Art:
The girl shook the child in the cradle, painting on canvas
by Lilia Kulianionak

Photograph of Kika Dorsey by Robin Enright Salcido

First Edition: August 2020

Pinyon Publishing
23847 V66 Trail, Montrose, CO 81403
www.pinyon-publishing.com

Library of Congress Control Number: 2020940410
ISBN: 978-1-936671-68-7

ACKNOWLEDGMENTS

The American Aesthetic: "Between You and Me"

Cleaver Magazine: "The Unborn"

Coldnoon: "Hunger," "The Eaten Valley," "Pregnant," "The Robin's Egg," "Three of Hearts"

The Copperfield Review: "Hunger"

The Indiana Voice Journal: "Everything Comes in Threes," "Journey to Lakes," "Thirst"

KYSO Flash: "All Grown Up Now," "A Bone in my Body," "Lightning Veins," "Polishing Leather," "Silhouettes," "The Voices," "The Walls"

The Indiana Voice Journal: "Everything Comes in Threes," "Journey to Lakes," "Thirst"

Narrative Northeast: "Lullaby," "Mother, My Ashes," "The Eaten Valley"

The Prism Review: "Cuckoo," "Hunger," "Monkshood," "Rheinwiesenlager"

The RavensPerch: "I Wish I Had"

S/tick: "The Savior"

Turtle Island Quarterly: "Blue"

for my mother

Hilda Bomer Stalzer

(1943 - 2016)

Contents

Foreword   1

VIENNA IS A BROKEN MAN

Hunger   7
Monkshood   8
Cuckoo   10
Leoben   12
Ingvild and the Soldiers   13
Polishing Leather   15
All Grown Up Now   16
Three of Hearts   17
Lord Haw Haw   18
Lullaby   20
The Robin's Egg   22
Pregnant   24
Marli   26
Rheinwiesenlager   28
Broken Back of Vienna   30
Run Dry   32
Marble Jew   34
I Never Cry   36
The Eaten Valley   38
The Voices   40
Hanna   42

DAUGHTER OF HUNGER

Aftermath   49
Lightning Veins   51
Easters   54
Krieglergasse   55
A Bone in My Body   58
Journey to Lakes   60
Blue   62
Angelika, the Daisies   65
Everything Comes in Threes   68
Silhouettes   70
The Unborn   72
I Wish I Had   74
Savior   76
My House   77
Mother, My Ashes   79
The Sunflowers   81
The Walls   83
Thirst   84
Between You and Me   86
Yellow   88

FOREWORD

My mother was born on June 17th, 1943, in Retz, Austria. Her family later moved to Leoben, a small city at the foot of the Alps, where my grandfather was a bureaucrat and my grandmother raised three children during and after the war until she died at the age of thirty-five, when my mother was nine years old. Growing up, I heard stories about the hardships of the post-war years; hunger dominated them. As a child, I grew tired of having to hear, as I ate a banana, how my mother had eaten her first one at the age of twelve when at a zoo with a richer child, who threw the fruit to the monkeys. My mother asked for the peel and ate it. She told the girl it was her favorite part. She also recounted foraging in the Alps for sustenance, and the day they ate the wrong kind of mushroom and grew very sick. She often fainted from malnourishment.

When my mother was dying of Alzheimer's, I began to forage for her memories as she lost them. I researched that era, and I began to collect more images and stories of the extreme hunger and poverty of the post-WWII years. Children were born from foreign soldiers, fathers disappeared, and hunger reigned. The people who pay the price for war are often innocent, especially the children.

Beyond the time period I didn't experience, I explored my own life with my mother and my father—who suffered from mental illness and committed suicide as my mother declined with Alzheimer's—as well as my own role as a mother and partner. I brought my mother back to the U.S. and managed her care for six years as I raised my young children. The broken man of Vienna extended to the literal broken body of my father on the cobblestone streets when he flew himself out of a window in Vienna, and the broken mother who forgot everything.

This book was written as a warning as much as a way to find closure and create words out of my mother's ashes. It brings to life a past that is all too present for many people on our planet, and it embraces the children and mothers who are just trying to take care of a delicate and fragile future, to watch their children grow.

Vienna is a Broken Man

HUNGER

I'm hungry all the time.
We forage in the Alps for mushrooms and elderberry blossoms
that we dip in cornmeal and fry from the butter
of a neighbor's cow.
The oak and beech disappear as I climb
further to fir, larch, and pine.
I pick edelweiss and arnica
to set in the blue glass vase on our table.
We eat the polenta with what we have gathered,
and Mutti is always angry,
Vati a traveling tailor and never around,
hungry stepchildren.

Once we accidently ate poisonous mushrooms.
I knew something was wrong when the August light
turned orange and from the faces of Russian soldiers
emerged black beetles,
and my brother lay holding his stomach and vomiting.

My stomach is full of knives.
It is an empty cavern
where my dead mother
dwells below budding breasts.

Sometimes I want to cross the River Mur
and never return.
Sometimes the river roils in my body
and I pull the sun into me.
Sometimes I see a golden eagle on the elm tree.
He looks royal,
as if he's won a war.

MONKSHOOD

I dress like a man to keep the soldiers away,
in lederhosen and my father's old red worn shirt
and I can smoke tobacco like any man
and with my father away, I can chop the wood
and bring in food, though money is scarce.

It is summer, and I forage in the mountains
for nettle and dandelion and mushrooms.
Mutti's joints ache all the time,
and I make her a poultice for her fingers.
I walk through the valley with monkshood,
its helmets of blue flowers blooming,
its deathly beauty like this summer after the war.
I collect valerian, thyme, and juniper berries
to help us sleep.

I don't sleep.
My friend Katarina carries the seed
of a Soviet soldier
who forced her to surrender under his hips.
They take our tobacco and schnaps,
and at night their loud, drunken forays
down our street frighten me.
I've started wrapping cotton strips from Vati's shirts
across my breasts to hide them.
Once a soldier grabbed the strap of my lederhosen
and brushed his hand across my breast,
leaned his sweaty face and onion breath toward me
and said something in Russian,
and I pulled away from him and ran home.

My mother told me the Goddess of the Moon,
Hecate, poisoned her father with monkshood.
I cup the blue flowers in my hand.
The sun is a father landing on us.
Some fathers are not to be trusted.
Vati had fed the soldiers on the front line,
that's all I know.
He left us to more soldiers, fathers of war.
Monkshood is why witches traverse the sky on brooms.
The sun is a giant who won't let us go.
When it dims there will be root,
and I will fly.

CUCKOO

They come to me for the schnaps,
which I distill from the pressed juice of my apples.
Thirty apple trees, not enough coal for winter,
autumn's harvest good,
husband disappeared in war.

When the trains from Vienna come,
I have my wares ready,
otherwise they hamster my goods away.
Today I traded six bottles of schnaps
for two pairs of shoes,
two liters for eighty horseradish roots,
six kilos of potatoes for a pair of working trousers,
two kilos of butter from my cow for two shirts,
and twenty cigarettes I pilfered from the soldier
while he slept next to me for two pairs of socks.
The shoes are too big for my son and me,
but the leather is strong,
and the shoes we have been wearing have torn soles.

But for the coal I gave up my father's gift to me
when I married, a cuckoo clock with a ceramic plate,
its wooden bird painted red and green
like the colors that will fade soon in our landscape.
It whistled every hour, spread its wings,
reminded me of spring,
reminded me that I was alive.
I gave that cuckoo the name of my brother, Hugo,
also lost to war.

Now it will only be the whistles of trains I listen for
to barter my wares,
give what the earth has given to me,
give the song of my brother away
to fill the stove with coal
and watch how the fire licks it and rises
and moves so fast as it flickers
like the second of an hour,
so fast that I can't keep up with it with my eyes,
coal as black as the market
now glowing through winter's cold.

LEOBEN

We used to trade iron in this city
and pride ourselves in the red and white Baroque facade
of Hacklhaus. The Gösser Kirtag was a street fair
with schnitzel and sauerkraut and semmel,
and the women were plump and danced to the accordion.

A bastard son later,
four children to my Nazi wife
who collects parakeets and has the iron hand
of the Austrian mines,
two sons too weak to till a garden,
I travel and sew the dirndls for a few groschens,
but mostly I repair the Russian soldiers' uniforms.
One man wanted a coin button
like the one on my wolljacke.
Another needed a torn lapel repaired.
Torn by a woman's hand, he said.

Sometimes I sew through thick leather
and I think of the animal,
whose tough meat we ate.

One day I caught my daughter
chewing the leg of my lederhosen.
I took it way and handed her a potato,
and she threw it in my face.

I wasn't angry.
I picked her up and carried her to the birds,
the blue parakeet singing in the waning

October light.

INGVILD AND THE SOLDIERS

She was six and lived in an old castle.
During the war there were no men, no fathers,
and when the women told her they were fighting,
she didn't understand.
The sirens were like the cry of wounded men,
and sometimes they woke her
when she dreamed about her mother sewing blouses
or dolls with capes,
red like raspberries sprinkled with sugar.

Later there were men in uniforms.
A German soldier once whittled a wooden doll for her
with a head scarf nailed on top,
and later the English soldiers gave her roses.
Close up the soldiers,
with their beards and cigarettes and uniforms,
did not scare her, but when she saw them
in the distance, silhouettes like shadows, they did.
Once she went into the woods to pick raspberries
and heard a noise.
She thought they were soldiers and her heart
skipped, but instead a deer crashed
through the forest, leaping among the brambles,
its coat the color of earth,
eyes big and black as an eclipsed moon.
Another time she looked up at a mountain
where the trees thinned out,
and thought the lone trees were Russian soldiers
coming down to take her away.

When the fighting came too close,
the war drove them from the castle.
Her mother buried their belongings in the box—
the precious teakettle with roses on it, the documents—
but she took the wooden doll with the head scarf and the nails.

Nails were like men,
the way they stood straight on the mountaintops,
the way they scattered when God spilled them as He built a mountain,
the way they held Jesus on his cross,
and sometimes she imagined her father holding the doll,
his arms thick like the branches of the ash tree
that stood bare in winter with nothing left to give
but hope for spring.

POLISHING LEATHER

At school she learned how to darn socks,
sew the skirts of dirndls,
make the dough for kartoffelknödel,
and polish the leather of shoes.
It didn't matter that they were poor,
five years later when the war ended and they were hungry—
she would still try to keep the shoes clean and shiny,
even after her son's was losing its sole
and she had no glue to fix it.
Her neighbor traded two kilos of apricots for new shoes,
but the fox snatched her chickens
and the Russians drank her schnaps
and she had nothing else to trade.

In the evening she set her shoes
near the door and rubbed cloth against them
until the black shined.
She brushed her long hair
and looked at herself in the mirror—
dark eyes of Slavic blood staring back at her—
and something told her to leave.
But they said it was no better in Vienna,
better to till one's own garden.

The next day she dug for carrots,
soil piling on her shoes,
brown like her eyes on the black leather,
all of it dark like the day the bombs fell
and her husband with his torn boots
climbed into the torn sky.

ALL GROWN UP NOW

I pick blossoms from the elderberry bushes in town,
their white flowers like the stars I wish on every night
to bring Vati home.
We used to dunk them in batter and fry them,
but now we have no flour,
so we just use the eggs from our chickens.
Mutti says the apple tree will bear us fruit
despite the spring hail.
She says we'll be fine,
but yesterday she was crying in the kitchen
while cutting potatoes.

I want to help my mother.
I collect coal and wood for the cold days
and I told her I would be the man of the house,
but that just made her cry again.

Once she set my brother down on the bed
and left him to boil water
and soak the diapers with vinegar and an egg
to cool his fever,
and he rolled to the side of the bed and almost fell off,
but I caught him.

I need to be sharp
like the knife Vati gave me for whittling,
though I haven't whittled anything since he left.
I need to keep my eyes wide open
like windows drinking this spring light,
like my brother's infant soul,
his cries as open as the white blossoms I collect.

THREE OF HEARTS

She did laundry for the Russian soldier,
his uniform rank with stale sweat and tobacco,
he towering so tall that his head
almost touched the ceiling of their home.
He had a beard and nicotine-stained fingers,
and he shared tobacco with her husband.
His German was halting like an old train,
and one day he told her that his wife in Russia
could not conceive, and he wanted to take Liesel,
their daughter, back to his country.
He was pulling kings as he played bauernschnapsen
with her husband, whose calloused hands pulled
a three of hearts.

Three, the number of her children,
she with a daughter completing the trinity
like clover leaves or the Holy Ghost
she sprinkled on herself at church.

"Nein," she would tell him, "Nyet,"
folding his starched shirt,
"She is our child."

It was a game he would never win.

LORD HAW HAW

He was searching for scraps of wood
near the Danish border of Germany,
reminiscing about his fame,
his broadcasts to the British and the Americans,
his attempts to steer them to the truth,
the darkness of the Jews,
the beauty of fascism in his body
warm like schnaps
that loosened his tangled mind,
unraveling prisons the way he extricated himself
from the bowels of Brooklyn
and now had a British passport, his healed broken nose,
and a scar on his cheek from brawling with the liberal swine.

Drunk, he picked up the scraps,
the way he had stolen scraps of news from the Allies
to give to the people, to watch their souls burn like his.
An officer nearby was searching the ground
and he said, "There are a few more pieces here,"
and the officer asked for his passport.
Drunk, Lord Haw Haw fumbled in his left pocket and gave him
the British one, his forged German papers in the right one.

So accustomed to gray skies,
the sun was a mouth that ate him.
A raven flew above the oak tree
and a squirrel leapt from a branch.
The officer shot Lord Haw Haw.
A bullet nestled in his leg, and he stared at a cloud
that looked like Hitler's angry face,
mustache where the cloud streaked gray.

In 1946 he would be the last war criminal
whom Britain would hang.

The rope coiled around his neck like a snake.
His white scar turned red, crooked nose a beak,
and he kicked his feet as if trying to run
from shadows he fashioned into borders,
from the bully in Brooklyn who sliced him with a bottle cap,
from the leaden sky of an ill spring.

The voice of Lord Haw Haw
disappeared beneath the raven wing
to emerge again and again,
like a whip of fire and fear,
its tail slicing countries in two.

LULLABY

She lived in a makeshift camp
in front of Vienna's ruined bahnhof.
Her feet were bare, and her filthy skin
itched as she wiped the lice from her dirty eyebrows.
Her brother hopped around the American canteen, clapping,
and the soldier threw him half a sandwich,
but the older boy Hans wrestled it away from him.

Yesterday was a better day.
A soldier threw her two cigarettes,
and she bartered them for two apples,
one for her and one for her brother.

At night she sometimes dreamed of her mother,
dead from an air raid in Essen,
her mother kneading the potato dough to make knödel,
her mother polishing their black shoes,
darning their socks.
Of Vati she remembered little.
He disappeared in Russia.
She remembered his shoulders, broad and strong
like a castle's stone.

In one dream her mother was a small bird
perched on the rubble.
Her hair crow-black,
she had no wings, just a coat of tattered feathers.
She sang to her daughter the lullaby
about the moon emerging from the clouds, blurred,
and the stars coming out,
and when the daughter awoke,

it was the middle of the night
and the soldiers were drinking
on the broken steps of the station,
speaking a language she didn't understand.

The moon was a sickle in the sky,
a scythe threshing the heavens for a song.

THE ROBIN'S EGG

I remember when they made me wear the yellow badge
and scrub the sidewalks,
even in the cold, even in the rain.

Before, my mother had lit the two candles
and recited the blessing of Shabbat over the challah bread,
braided as my mind was then,
my father's hair black above his dark eyebrows,
my sister picking at her fingernails,
I thinking about Inge and whether she liked me,
how she gave me a glass of fresh grape juice that day
when the synagogue wasn't destroyed.
It was spring and I found an abandoned robin's nest
and kept the blue egg.

Mother says we're lucky.
Hugo hid us in the cellar,
the bombs are over,
and the swastika on the temple is now rubble,
and we can't eat kosher because we have to eat
whatever we can get.

Yesterday a Russian soldier gave me a potato
he roasted on a fire near the Stadttempel
and I gave it to my sister,
but she insisted that I eat the peel.

I look for Inge.
Mother said she was taken away.
I still see her as the beautiful Bat Mitzvah,
with her peach gown.

I kept the robin's egg.
It's in a box I hid under the bed in the basement.
I wonder what happened to the mother.
I wonder how long it took
for the chick in its blue home to die.

PREGNANT

Adam left when the spring rain
dampened the rubble they still hadn't cleared
across the street.
My belly is swollen with his baby,
that dark American with eyes and skin like chocolate,
arms of muscle from helping us clear rubble,
his hair rough on my hands.
Mutti said she wouldn't talk to me
for carrying a negerkind,
and Vati never returned from Russia.

Adam said he would come back for me
and take me to Chicago,
to his home on the South Side where
they play the blues in small bars
like the music they played when we danced
and drank schnaps.
The lake stretches for miles, he said,
just like the ocean, and he would fish for sturgeon for us,
and he said I could teach his mother how to make spätzle.
He said the lake is so big you can't see the other side,
and now my vision is blocked by rubble and ruins,
and Vienna is a broken man,
a crippled shadow of what it was,
and I want to sew for my baby but there is no thread—
only the spring rains thread the sky—
and sometimes I'm just so tired.

Mutti told me once she made potato dumplings
and I wouldn't stop eating them,
and I vomited.

She told me not to climb the ash tree
and I did, and I fell.
I've never been able to see the other side,
and now my future I wrap around the waxing moon
of my body and these days the clouds won't part
but when they do, the city is darker now,
and you can see the scintillation of stars like city lights,
like Vienna when he sang and the boats
on the Danube carried gold.

I imagine Adam's looking at the same stars in Chicago,
and one is so tiny it fits inside of me,
in my small lake of flesh.

MARLI

We lived in a small wooden house in Frankfurt,
Mutti, Oma, and I.
I was born from a Russian soldier, Grischa,
who lived with them after the war.
They did his laundry, fed him, sewed his worn uniform.
My mother went with him to bars
where they drank schnaps and danced.
When Mutti was heavy with me in her belly, he left
to transport Russian soldiers to the Ukraine.
Mutti never heard from him again.

My mother was a sunset on a winter day.
My mother was wounded in a different way than the soldiers,
and when she grabbed my arm to drown us in the River Oka,
there was no harvest that year,
and I had a bee sting on my thumb that throbbed
and I cried, pulling myself away,
and ran home.
The day I was to marry
Mutti locked herself in the kitchen,
turned on the gas stove,
and curled in a corner.
We found her and then we said our vows.

I seek my father,
but the German Red Cross says
they only search for German soldiers.
But I won't give up.
On my mother's deathbed,
after years of silence, she told me of him,
finished all the bits of whispers I caught as a child,

his dust on her breath, all the strands
I wove into dreams when the nights were cold
and I needed him the most.

On New Years I make zakuska, pickle cabbage,
put it in a jar with berries, salt, and spices,
and we eat it with salmon caviar on toast and vodka.
I read Dostoevsky,
punishment and crime like what I was born to
after the war, after the dusty cellar lost our bodies.

I wish I could talk to my father,
ask him how he celebrated Christmas,
whether they put candles and gingerbread on trees like we do.
This year I lit the candles and sang "Silent Night"
and thought how the silence seeps into my days,
and I wrap absence around me like a shawl,
and sometimes not knowing keeps you warm,
and sometimes I want to feel the bite of the cold.

RHEINWIESENLAGER

We sleep on wooden beds,
blocks of wood for pillows.
It's June and I think of home,
of how the apple trees must be blooming
and the cows calving.
For dinner we eat cans of beans and stale bread,
sometimes half of a potato.

In April we were outside in an open field on the Rhine
with no shelter, so we dug holes with spoons
and tin cans, and the rain
made the holes collapse, holes
where we tried to take shelter.
Willy died in one.
After that, I gave up.

Yesterday I woke up and my neck
felt as if daggers were piercing it.
I couldn't turn my head to the left.
The Americans had stolen the wristwatch
my father had given me,
a gold watch with a black face and golden hands
that told me what time it was throughout the war,
which for years felt as if it would have no end.
I felt for the watch and brushed across my empty wrist.
The soldiers pulled us out of bed,
draped hoods on us,
and said they were sending us to the gallows.

I walked with my sore neck and feet
with toenails of fungus and legs aching

and thought of the apple trees, my daughter,
my two sons, the people I've killed,
the women I've loved, wienerschnitzel with lemon,
and yellow boletus mushrooms we dunked in batter
and fried in butter. I thought of the time
my brother and I stole my father's cigarettes
and tried to smoke them in the park,
how the tobacco seared my lungs
and I became dizzy and coughed.
I thought how I wanted a cigarette.

They made me stand on the platform to hang.
They laughed and let me down.

That night it rained,
water falling like a latticework of stars,
and I thought of the swastika like the bent hands
of a watch spinning forward,
like the bent spine of a dying man.

Yesterday I died,
and one day I will do it again,
and I may never again taste those apples,
but I hope my children do.
I hope they slice them and open their mouths to the rain,
and I hope they forget me.

I have forgotten myself already.
I have remembered too much already.

BROKEN BACK OF VIENNA

Mutti told me to go out and find the American soldiers, to see if I can bring back some food like their cracker biscuits, my favorite. I just turned twelve and now I am the man of the house.

I go to Heinrichshof, the apartment buildings across from the opera, where soldiers sometimes congregate to help clear the rubble and try to find the bodies buried there. A girl with matted raven-black hair runs to me, thinking my empty bag has food, and tries to trade three cigarettes. I hold my hands out to show I have nothing. I don't recognize her. Is she the little girl who held her mother's hand that day, the one with the yellow dress?

I think I smell a fire so I follow my nose, because soldiers build fires where they cook potatoes and drink, so my nose leads me down broken streets. Rubble. Blackened stone. Crushed vehicles. A skinny brown dog that shies from me. People roaming, their eyes yellow with blood shot through them. Shattered glass. I turn down one street and then another, and nothing looks the same when the bombs digest a city.

My hollow belly leads me toward the smoke. A pigeon lands on a broken windowsill. The sky is leaden. My mind is a handful of crumbs that the birds are eating, crumbs that should turn into flight where I can look down on this city and map the maze, but the birds can't fly. They are dying. Flightless sparrow in my path. Smoke ahead of me.

I turn a corner and see the fire. Soldiers haul rubble from the middle of the street. A black one looks at me, his face sooty like the wood we burn, and says something I don't understand, and I hold my hands out to him. He gives me canned cheese, gum, three cans of sausage, and a bar of chocolate.

I think of the time my mother told me to polish my shoes and I threw all the mushrooms drying on the kitchen table to the floor, and I wonder whether she has forgiven me for being so thankless because I can't forgive myself. Then I turn back home with my bag of food and the sky is dimming, fire glowing deeper orange, streets before me like letters I cannot decipher, like the soldiers' languages. I head down a street, crooked broken back of Vienna, and I am lost.

RUN DRY

She lies in bed shaking, covered in sweat.
She could have sworn she'd hid it in the stocking drawer,
but every time she looks, it's gone.

Stumbling out of bed in the dark, she holds
her arms out, gropes toward the dresser to look again,
opens the third drawer, fingers
through the thin sheer of her panty hose.
Nothing.

They were never bombed.
Nights in the cellar were warmer with schnaps,
and she had her bottles hidden for years
from her husband, hoarded them
like the city rat that she was—
        one under the bed,
        one behind the couch,
        one in the stocking drawer.
But now they are gone and she doesn't remember
drinking them all but she doesn't remember
much anyway, snippets lost to a haze
like the stumbling images of dreams that sicken
her in her hung-over mornings—
        rodents in a cage she forgot to feed so the mothers eat
            their babies,
        a trip to Leoben to visit her brother but the train derails
            and the soldiers come and take her son,
        sirens wailing, but she can't move her feet because she is
            paralyzed so she thinks this is it, she will die.

Then she remembers.
Once she went to the market and bought Irish whiskey,
and she stashed it behind the smoked mackerel in the cellar.

She descends,
dim morning light dissipating in the gray stone,
cellar with all its ghosts,
and behind the cans she finds it—
     warm amber like the earrings her husband had given her,
     malty smell of soil and nuts,
     bite on her tongue to drug her tremors away and leave her
          with warm legs, warm fingers,

and nothing more to hide.

MARBLE JEW

I spend my pfennigs on marbles.
It's spring and the elderberry and apple trees are blooming
and I buy marbles for a pfennig where Frau Stalzer works.
She helps me choose them,
and once she set aside a glass marble,
blue and white like an ocean below wispy clouds.

The boys like to play marble pyramid.
We set three marbles down
and balance a fourth on top,
and if the boys knock it down,
they get to take it with the marbles
that rolled past the pyramid.

I stack it and make sure I don't press the base too hard
into the ground so they don't call me a "Marble Jew."
But I won't give up the blue one.
Hans leans over and says, "Use that one,"
and I shake my head,
and he calls me a Marble Jew.

My legs become icicles,
my hands tremble like the light beneath blooming trees,
and when I look at my friends,
I see the crumbled wall that lies where the synagogue had been,
rubble in their eyes below a greedy sun.

That night at dinner I count my marbles
and think about how much I'm willing to give up.
I roll the blue one across my palm.
It's the color of my veins

that travel through my body like trains.
There is no one in them but me,
and I am so alone.

I NEVER CRY

The milk is coming in.
Speckled frost on walls like stars,
coal running out so we can't boil water
to soak comfrey compresses for my sore breasts.

I named her Eva,
my baby who knew paradise in my womb,
now born to this—
the broken Adam of Vienna,
the only father she will ever have.

I have felt the tremor of bombs in the shelter
where we sweated to the thunder.
I have traded my grandmother's ring
for six kilos of potatoes.
I have nursed Michi, the friend with me
in the darkness of our ruined home,
when she coughed all night,
fever flushing her face like fire to a wick.
Now Michi nurses me.
She cut Eva's cord.

It was snowing.
The baby came so fast that when
I pulled her to me,
she fell asleep in my arms.
She looked like my mother,
her nose a claw, black hair.
I held her warm thin body,
delicate skin,
and she never cried.

I never cry.
It's not for the lack of melancholy or grief.
It may be the hunger.
Our tears are drowned by the Danube
that seeks the Black Sea.

I wonder why it's black.
Maybe the floor is so dark,
so deep,
that no one can touch it.

THE EATEN VALLEY

She told the three Russian soldiers
she would gather snails that day,
and she picks their brown and white shells
from the dew-drenched land,
and in her satchel she has three,
and Mutti said to try to find a dozen,
to feed her
and her sister
and the three soldiers
who track mud in their home,
setting Mutti's face into grim lines.

The gentian is in bloom,
deep blue petals curling, surrounding yellow stamen
like a fallen sun,
like the hole inside of her
where her older brother and father disappeared,
hole like the caves where the ibex live
high near tundra, young ones with velvet horns
soft like her before the war,
the hunger and the blood that comes now
every month, and the soldiers with
their laundry
and tobacco
and vodka
and thirsty eyes.

She comes to a meadow with a snow gum
that survived the fire,
its new sprouts reaching from the blackened trunk
like a womb, bulbous.

Out of every death sprouts an insistence
to live, despite the ashes, despite the eaten valley,
and she thinks of a day when maybe she will stretch herself
like alpine tundra's five petals—
                her brother with his mucous breath,
                her vati of yellow nicotine hands,
                her mutti of yellow yarn for socks
                her breasts aching like sunset when the moon
                      begins to bulge,
                her sister the petal that finishes the cross with her
                      body, hungry,
and all the petals
will drink in the sun as if never losing it,
never to be buried by the winter frost.

THE VOICES

Helmut's father was an engineer in 1944,
constructed highways, a socialist in Vienna
who gave his family a nice apartment
and enough money to buy
artichokes and oranges at the Naschmarkt.

Helmut was four years old and always liked the cellar
where they descended when the sirens blared,
the cellar where the children played cards.

His father listened to the wireless,
which was forbidden.
One day the air pressure from nearby bombs broke it,
and Helmut saw glass shards and wires strewn on the floor,
and he didn't understand what happened to the humans
who lived in it with the voices of war.
He expected them to crawl out of the shards,
those voices from lands where soldiers fought,
his own home a shelter for them,
the instrument through which they spoke to his father,
a man who built highways
where they wouldn't travel until later,
until the war pushed them to the countryside
where the women hid in a shed from Russian soldiers.

They were not allowed in the shed.
His baby brother cried too much.
They would go to the woods
and build a shelter out of sticks and bramble.

A voice can be broken into pieces.
His baby brother had too much voice.
Sometimes a voice can stop as quickly
as the boy's heart they'd found hanging
from a tree after he had stepped on a mine.
Sometimes a voice lives on for many decades
after the body crawls out of the ruins,
after the war.
Sometimes a child finds joy despite the ruins,
and in the summer the sun blankets the bodies,
as it always has,
and the chestnut trees bloom.

HANNA

We live in the Von-Viertel,
the aristocratic quarter of Potsdam,
now full of mines, shattered cars,
buckled bridges, and rubble.

I take care of my teenage children,
dress my daughter as a boy and cut off her long plaits
to save her from the Russians,
who throw grenades into the river,
their form of angling,
and roast the fish in fires.

People hunt for booty,
and we lost eight watches and all our bicycles.
My son traded our cuckoo clock for a bike,
rusted with white peeling paint,
but that too got stolen.
Time became the long days of foraging
and waiting with no hands to show us a way out.

One day I brought home a section of a dead horse
and marinated it in vinegar and spices.
Another day I had a share of a cow
that had trodden on a mine.
Once in the waters of Hasengraben
were the contents of a cellar,
and we waded in its water and brought back
wine that we traded for bread and bacon.

They said the Americans were coming so we waited.
The food was running out,

so we ate potato flakes and the fruit and vegetables
from abandoned gardens,
and once I dodged Russian bullets to steal
twenty-five kilos of potatoes that they were saving
to distill for their vodka, which they drank like water.

My teenage children are long and lanky
and they grow despite the hunger.
Their lives were royal;
now they are scavengers like the crows
that live on our beech tree
and caw at me when I take the dead squirrel from them
and cook it with carrots.

I was once a Jew until I converted to Protestantism.
I liked the story of Golem in synagogue,
that creature born of mud,
and now parts of it cover my boots,
worn from roaming the land for food,
and I've forgotten the Hebrew letters
to animate this death and bring it to life.

I press my head against the earth
on a warm spring morning,
May-green grass against my cheek,
and my daughter carries her blue satchel
to go scavenging,
and she asks me what I am doing.
I think of the waltz that brought my husband and me
together before the war,
and the earth yields no music,

but it carries me, the small Jewish girl—and I say,

I'm listening.

Daughter of Hunger

AFTERMATH

She has been gone a long time,
thirteen years since her memory failed her
and her language became crumbs for the sparrows,
since she dangled her feet in the Danube and fed ducks
and gazed at the blooming chestnut in the Prater.
Six years since she roamed the green hallways
of the Memory Unit and stole fake pearls and photos
from the other residents' rooms.
Two years since she walked hunched and unsteady
and skimmed her hands to the walls to keep from falling,
and two years of falling.

She was born in 1943 during the war,
when Nazis saluted their leader
and sullied the word for heal—*heil*,
when bombs tore through cities and wrenched
the skies of salvation, emptied stomachs
of all but fear.
In the spring of 1945 it ended,
a cold spring with hail,
and my mother toddled through the house
and sat on the Russian soldier's lap,
who sang her songs and ran his fingers through her curls.
She grew despite her hunger.
She tasted foreign lands and languages.
She stretched herself across an earth
pocketed with bomb craters.

I empty the room of her belongings—
stale-smelling clothes, cards from friends
she was unable to read,

paintings of fruit and flowers
and portraits of my father and sisters
and me at eleven.
Her hairbrush is full of gray hair,
and I pull out the oily strands,
some as white as snow.
I think of white, the same as black,
that blank sheet on which we sketch,
in which we dream in the shadows,
the bluntness of death our backdrop,
our curtain. I think how I will miss my mother,
how I've missed her for years.

LIGHTNING VEINS

The veins in my hand are shaped like a tree,
and one on the inside of my arms is a lightning bolt.
I remember my father's translucent skin,
his blue veins visible through a pale, transparent body.
I used to think I was too much like him,
thin-skinned and delicate,
fragile as a thin vase holding
daisies I bought for my mother
in the spring hail of Vienna.

My father accused me of stealing his music that day.
We were in the small living room,
tall ceilings, black piano where he sat,
ruffling pages of music,
I on the white couch,
Turks yelling on the cobbled streets below,
onion and paprika of goulash in the air,
Father pointing to me, saying
Who told you to do it?

I always believed in porous borders,
Syrians now in Vienna
after crossing tumultuous waters into Greece,
refugees from Mexico trudging through Arizona's desert,
my hands that sometimes bleed,
a nightmare swimming from deep waters
into the struggling world
and sometimes the dream
or the daffodil rises from the earth's border
in the spring, a bulb we never planted.

Father, this spring it didn't hail.
I wish you could see it.
Apple blossoms promising fruit,
soft rain that the grass drinks.

I left the apartment that day,
frightened and shaking after he grabbed my arm
and insisted on my crime.
I rode the streetcar round and round the Ring,
sitting on a wooden seat
with a muzzled Shepherd
and punks eating gelato.
I got off at Schwedenplatz
and walked to Stephanskirche,
stared at wooden Jesus on the cross and cried,
my flesh wet and burning from the hail.

He climbed off the cross that day.
He traced the lightning bolt
on the inside of my arm
and he brought water to the city.

I stole my father's music ten years later,
after he died,
and I made it my own,
becoming the criminal I never was,
sleeping in the dissonant notes of jail
and bleeding across borders to find my home,
far away from him,
though I carry him in my skin—
rivers of veins blue-green like the Danube,

rivers I sometimes dare to cross,
rivers that flood when the sky is too heavy,
lightning etched
in the spring sky.

EASTERS

I

It's Easter and I paint my nails powder-blue and eat deviled eggs. I call my old boyfriend, leave a message, and pull on a jacket when the clouds roll in. I hide plastic Easter eggs filled with confetti at a neighbor's house, where I talk to a nurse who obsesses on her health. I clean the drawer with broken crayons when I come home, and I pick ticks off the dog. I look at our lone daffodil and don't pluck it. I buy irises and stick my nose in them to breathe their sweet breath. I cough because I'm sick with a spring cold and go outside to pick up sticks from the willow, set them in a pile, and then read a book with alligators in it. I drink a shot of whiskey. I'm sitting on my green couch, and it is torn but it is mine.

II

It was Easter again and again and my mother baked ham, my father was always dying, and my sisters and I squabbled. The maple tree housed squirrels and blue jays. It was sunny, or it was raining. We went to church to learn about resurrection. I thought about my friends as the preacher droned on, or I thought about how my history teacher didn't like me, or I thought about the white mice my science teacher fed the boa, or I thought about sex. We ate jellybeans and played marbles. We ate chocolate bunnies and played jacks. My father lay on the couch so we sat on the floor. It had a design of flowers and a castle. There were no faces on the rug, not one eye to watch over us as we played to win and sometimes lost.

I was on the floor like a beetle. I was on the floor like a fallen seed. I was a queen with no throne, sitting on the floor because my father would not rise.

KRIEGLERGASSE

It's the cobblestoned street of the warrior,
where my parents lived on the third floor
of an apartment building with stone steps
worn and dark from centuries of feet climbing.
My father drank wine and Vienna's music
in rooms with chandeliers and velvet.
My mother taught Mormons German
and fed the wood ducks on the Danube canal.
She slept through May's hail, a sky exhaling ice
falling on me as I rode my bike.
She woke to find parts of her missing—
buttons lost that had closed a memory into a body,
thread coming undone from the spool,
tangled on their floors.

Father was visiting the preacher ladling out Jesus.
He was starving himself.

I watched them,
how their train slipped off the tracks of their world,
derailed, tilted, jolting to a stop,
how my father's Jesus gave him a handful of nails,
the city cleaned the black soot off of Stephanskirche
and the tourists ambled into Schönbrunn
to learn about Queen Elizabeth,
her hair long, thick, and pendulous,
so dark like Vienna's woods.

Once I visited them and my mother couldn't play
backgammon anymore, the back chips confounding,
the stripes too parallel for her jagged mind.

My children were young.
My husband called me and told me
the dog had killed our blue parakeet, Indigo.
The children cried.
I bought them baklava from the Turks.
I spun that evening, waltzing at a ball
wearing a green velvet dress
in a city where warriors laid down weapons and sang.
I ran along the canal where men trained Shepherds to attack,
their bodies crashing into the padded pillows
dangling from a chestnut tree,
vicious warriors of a Vienna
that broke for me,
shattered into splinters made of my mother's gold crown
and my father's dissonant black key
from a piano he stopped playing.

The chestnut blooms survived May's hail.
I returned to Colorado.
I bought a new bird.
She was tiny and white.
She sat on my shoulder when I mopped my floors
in a house in my country
that nested half of me.

The other half was in Vienna.
It was made of shade, green threads, and the Vienna woods
where I gathered nettles and chanterelles.
I left the poisonous mushrooms to the earthen floor.
Others hunted the wild boar.
We ate them as medallions, round and peppered

with the mushrooms sautéed in butter,
pillows from the rich soil of the forest
that only grow in the shadows.

A BONE IN MY BODY

The willow stands guard over our house,
leaves like small knives and autumn's
breath touching it only to abandon
the dark bark in its inhale.
A rabbit sits hunched next to the lavender
and bindweed strangles the clematis.

I used to weed but I injured my knee,
bend and kneel to nothing—not even
my shrine with my father's gold pocket-watch,
my mother's garnet, and the quartz rock from my daughter.
I lie under the cross that nailed me to this world
with all its breath and rust and emptying wombs.

I used to want you
the way the garden wants rain.
Now highways beckon me,
there is a bone in my body I want to set fire to,
and yesterday my uncle died,
a man who played bridge and kissed everyone

right on the lips.
He sang me songs he made up for me when I was a child,
singing that TWA airlines stood for "Train with Air,"
or silly Austrian jingles,
and I would touch his rough face and laugh.
I place on the shrine the king of hearts.

I want you
the way a desert wants night, craving
stars, a relief from the sun that covers

the constellation of Pisces,
its water and its gray and its arching fish,
that water that lives in my body

in its eggs and winding veins
like the highways I don't travel,
the sink of the roots,
or the tangled branches of the willow insisting,
despite the heavy snow that will soon arrive,
to touch the sky.

JOURNEY TO LAKES

My lover and I drove the blue Volkswagen Beetle.
I had a green sleeping bag.
We slept next to highways on the dirt of Wyoming,
in parks in Idaho, where we woke up
                to sprinklers soaking us.
We picked corn from the fields of Iowa
                and roasted them in fires.
We slept on stone slabs along Lake Superior,
its cold water licking our feet when the sun rose.
I swam and swam.

My father was alive then,
but the ravens flew over Indiana
and my mother lost her memory.
We visited them in a cabin on Lake Michigan.
I ate peaches and collected blue beach glass.
You combed my sister's brown hair.
Ravens perched on lush maples
and the lake was as rippled
as my mother's dreams.
On the other side of her was a planet
                where no one could breathe.
On the other side of him was a methane lake
                he drank like rain.

I said to you if you touch me,
                you better learn to swim.
You collected stones and built me a wall.
Three sheep lived behind it.
One we sheared for the cold winter.
One we slaughtered in November.

One we kept to eat the thistle.

Our journey ended.
I had a bouquet of raven feathers.
You torched the beach glass
              and crafted a vase.

Three decades later my father died.
All I do anymore is swim.
One day I will learn to breathe underwater.

BLUE

My roaming is a birdless wing
that lands on the railroad tracks where I used to walk,
where the chain-link fences
held growling dogs
and some houses were blue,
ours too brick, too harsh.

I was missing my body,
my blue veins traveling to the heart.
I said I have no heart for this
when the preacher held up the crucifix
and I dreamed of powerful men with loins
of steel, not hands of nails,
not all that death.
I had enough of it,
Father on the couch
crazy as wingless birds
hopping on a desert floor
with hawks hunting.
They're always hunting,
I counting railroad ties
to measure how far
I was willing to travel from home,
pretending they were miles,
each one a wing I made into a garland,
blue wings I could set
on my dreams away from my parents' scrutiny,
away from the grout sealing brick
crumbling in acid rain.

I walked to a statue of St. Francis.
He was feeding a deer with birds on his shoulders
and he became my patron saint
in the convent where women gave up
sex for psalms and I roamed
with my dog, his gray body
like something trying to be shadow
but the light filtered through
the mesh of that piece of sky overhead
leaking, raining down what I lost in prayer
because I always asked
for what no one could give.

So feathers became foibles,
wings were wanton and whipped
in the wind of Midwestern storms
that sent us into the basement
of our brick house
and my parents laid down a bed for me.
I slept through the thunder,
trusting the heavens still
although it hid a sky,
it hid a haven of blue
and later it hid my children
who stopped following me long ago
though I still pray for them
to collect nails
and paint their houses blue
because it's the color that can sleep
and I want them to sleep better than I

and I want them
to see the train coming
and step off the tracks.

ANGELIKA, THE DAISIES

I'm thinking of you as Easter approaches
and the birds sing even before the sun rises.
How is Vienna?
I wish I were there to see the chestnuts bloom
in the Prater, though I'm sure it's still cold.
We north-dwellers always have to wait
so long for summer.

Yesterday the kids had no school
because a young woman from Miami
came to Denver, bought a gun,
and threatened schools, prowling
near Columbine.

Angelika, America is crazy.
America is that girl who eventually ran
in the woods naked and shot herself.
Now the children will return to schools
with doors guarded by armed cops.
There are so many guns.

I remember Vienna in April.
I ate baklava and watched my kids
swing and climb up to the high slide
in the Prater, the Turks picnicking,
the dogs romping on the green lawn.
I saw a long-haired Weimeraner
for the first time and it made me miss Char,
the family dog my parents left behind
in the states, to a farm with a colt born

to my mare, that roan I stopped riding when boys
became more interesting.

Last time I saw you my parents were dead.
My daughter learned the lines of the U-Bahn
and wandered the city as I gazed at Klimt's gold.
You and Heimo took us to the Wachau where
we ate dumplings with apricot and wandered
on the cobbled stone of villages.
The Danube was so in love with its riverbed
that it hummed, and Heimo told me
he had pancreatic cancer.
I felt the river's pull
crush my heart to its floor.
That day was the last day I saw my uncle.

You gave me a pendant of an orange stone
with a gold spiral.
I still haven't bought a chain for it.
Maybe I'll do that this week.
It will have to be gold.
I usually wear silver because it's less precious,
and gold is like the light of autumn,
and Angelika,
I've started fearing winter, the death of it.

But now it's spring and I'm wondering if they're
selling daisies yet at the market.
I remember buying a bouquet on Mother's Day
for my mother there when she was alive,
then riding my bike to their apartment.

It hailed on me, but the flowers remained intact.
Their white petals were like fingers
turning the page toward summer.

I hope you buy yourself some daisies.
If I were there, I'd buy some for you.

EVERYTHING COMES IN THREES

Three days since we lost our lamb
        to the wolf on the moors of England,
three sheep we brought into the barn,
whistling at our dogs
        and squinting in spring light,
three fingers you lost to war,
and three men who brought you down.

I can see the horizon from the plane's window.
I wonder how high do I have to climb
        to see it curve,
thinking of those lines of your body,
my hands wrapped around your thigh,
your eyes etched by the shadows of fire.

The wings are gray and covered in droplets,
and three men ask me where I'm going,
their questions like the fishing lines
        where we caught the sturgeon
and one line broke
and the fish got away,
        hook in its gray mouth.
I look at the gray wings
        and into the eyes of the three men
and I say,

wherever the crow can fly,
        to my father's grave in Tennessee,
        to the castle in London,
        to the bahnhof in Berlin,
wherever my lover buried me,

*where I rose and pushed open the coffin
and dug my way up,
shook off the dirt,
stole crumbs from the crows
and gathered their shed wings
                    into a bouquet*

*of the sex that brought me down,
the children who threw me roses,
and the body that climbed fire.*

SILHOUETTES

I am collecting silhouettes. The light behind them comes from a winter sky. They have sharp edges and cut my hands if I'm not careful, and their blackness blankets me when the nights grow cold. They are as silent as the snow and naked willow.

I have a broken mailbox, and I wonder if he forgot to write or whether the wind took his words away. He was color—hair of paprika, blue jeans and a shirt so green you could eat it. I think I loved him. Now he wanders the jungles of Borneo and collects macaques for the zoo, and I sit at home in black and white like Bacall and Bogart, always sparring with my world.

Once it was summer and we rode horses on the prairie and the horseflies kept biting us, our hands swatting them and my mind leagues under the sea, breathing water and touching purple sea fans. I was like that, always dwelling where I wasn't. He pointed across a yellow cornfield and said, *Look,* and all I saw was the sun sinking, streaks of pink and orange cloud streaks, and I wondered if I missed something, if he could see behind the light.

The silhouettes have no names and they dance behind a white screen when I let them go. One of them fought me and still my hands bleed, but I laid him down and his black lips touched me and he crawled, then stood, then stretched across the world like sorrow, and I watched him disappear, and I did nothing to stop him. I bandaged my hands and wrapped light across my eyes just so I could see color. I watched the dark dance of the others and pined for him.

Now the bulbs in the earth stir and it is almost spring. When I look at the ground, I begin to see green. There is another fight in my head, bitter words against sisters like sharp sea coral and I in that sea when only mountains rise before me, and I think of him again, his hair like fire, and I think of leaving, but there is no place to go when my mind does it all, and my body carries all the shadows of the world.

THE UNBORN

They are cutting down all the trees for Christmas.
Pine and spruce lie bundled on warehouse floors,
and I drink cognac in the corners of silent rooms,
red oriental rugs bursting with flowers and leaves,
warm feet wrapped in wool,
my body a river where the man capsized,
my body that I gave away,
all of it.

Cradled in me were three babies:
        one a riverbank where the father crawls,
        one the mica embedded in stone,
        one was never born,
and it is Christmas,
fields of stumps and birth of my son
on the frozen ground
and we unwrap trees
and cover them with tinsel and lights.

I never meant to make land fallow.
I believed in kind fathers.
I believed sons were gods
and my daughter would give birth to me.

I pulled them both out of me.
I cut their cords and heard them cry.
They grew in moonlight.
My son lost his boat.
My daughter glinted in stone and rose.

The unborn one reached high from seed and water,
and I hung on her a bulb.
It was silver.
It was mine.

I WISH I HAD

I woke up to cat food scattered on the floor
and the sun rising exhausted in dead winter,
fingering the ground with its orange light,
and babies sleeping,
heat humming like habit,
nicotine-stained hands stroking my black dog,
train whistling departure,
pillow with green flowers and coffee stains.

I woke up and threw off the covers,
blankets of grief blanketing the dream I had
where you were bathed in the red light
of a bar in Austria, and we were waiting
in line, holding carabiners, ropes, and harnesses
for the mountains we would climb.
When my eyes opened,
you disappeared,
and I knew you were never coming back.

I woke up but not really,
sleep lodged in my mind like my trunk
full of pictures, pictures of you in Memphis,
smiling in front of the white screened porch,
your freckles like stars.

I woke up to the sound of silence,
its cradled voice like your closed lips
when I asked you to come live in America,
and the Danube was full of swans,
and my children played with its stones.

I never really woke up.
I dreamed of the Black Sea
and ships on the Danube carrying coal
for that silver stove of ours,
where I cook you your last meal.

I never cooked your last meal,
but I wish I had.

SAVIOR

You said your climbing ladders
was a way to hang me
on the red dawn of ambition,
that every father is dead,
every son a climber,
and I said I never chose to live with
sacrifice,
and now all I know is loss.
I said, *Hush,*
my fingers tracing your lips,
wondering how the crucifix
you held in your pocket
showed no red blood,
its weathered wood smooth to my fingers
that slid down and took it out,
traced its dust,
and threw the savior
into the red fire.

MY HOUSE

My house sits heavy on my shoulders.
I've muscled my way across lakes
and pushed babies out of me,
whom I set in the kitchen of my house
next to blenders, highchairs, torn towels
and the attic I save for my dreams.

I walk with my house on my shoulders to a drugstore.
They sell me pills that only I can swallow—
made of strands of my mother's hair,
my father's sharp teeth, my sister's
dolls, and a white powder of promises
from God's mouth, pledges
of golden corn and rain.
I swallow the pills and dream in the dark
of my house floating on the sea,
an old man on the roof fishing.
When he catches one, he sets it on my lap
and I am hungry but the fish has eyes like mine
so I throw it back to the sea. I am thirsty
but the sea is salt so I let it feed the waves.
I am a mother so I am hungry and thirsty,
and the Holy Ghost of my house has no wings
but windows where I can watch the rain.

I wake up every day to the house pressing me,
and I rise with its roof of mind and basement
of feet, of ancestors and memory. I trudge
under its weight, searching for a land
where I can set it down, where I won't

crush a harvest or block a prairie dog burrow,
and I keep going, my spine bowing,
blackbirds chortling as if it were always dawn,
as if the sun needs to be called home.

MOTHER, MY ASHES

My house burned and now your ashes are mingled
with those of my home—
beds and scraps of poetry and walls.
The April skies are a blue hum that turns to gray water
when the winds come, and the bindweed
already strangles the yellow columbine while I let it,
while I seek shelter.

Mother,
if you were here I would lean against
your strong Austrian bones, touch
your weathered face and remind you
that every home is temporary, even that of body,
and you didn't have to fight your death so much,
the ragged breathing and sweat in the nursing home,
which smelled like detergent and urine.

Mother,
if you were here you would find me a home.
I am so alone.
But I have friends and family, just not you.
In the evenings the liquor soothes me,
and when the sun drops over the mountains,
shadows stretch into my belly and nestle
in my empty breasts that once fed my children,
as you did me.
I become the rain and though the ground is thirsty,
I want the sun to cut through the trees and allow
the shade to do its dark work.

Father gave me a pill made of blood and rancor
and he told me if I swallow it, an apple tree
would grow in my body.
He gave me a glass of water and made me swallow it,
and you didn't protect me.
It tasted like vinegar and metal.
It grew in me and God pushed me out of the jungle
into a city's alley where discarded needles
punctured my feet and the man with the green coat
gave me a torn blanket.
At least now I'm never cold.
I forgive you.

Mother,
I remember how your ashes glinted warm on the Danube
and carried you to the Black Sea.

The only sea I know is the Sargasso Sea,
which has no shore.

THE SUNFLOWERS

It is always morning and black before the sun rises,
a braided, rippled river of sleep untangling in coffee

and I am covered with a blanket made from the wool
of sheep I lost count of and memories I saved in a hickory box

my father gave to me from the mental hospital.
He shellacked it with a scene from a magazine

of a horse grazing with a red barn in the background.
It was like the barn he would take me to on his Harley

where I rode my wild horse that bucked off everyone but me,
my horse Sandy with her roan coat and half-Arab foal.

And now it is dark morning and I've lost the box
where I stored my pearls and red rabbit foot keychain

for luck I managed to have enough of in life, and I never
used the amulet for keys because we never locked our doors.

Now all I have of my father is a painting by my mother
of his freckled face surrounded by sunflowers, and as I sip

coffee I think of the day I walked up the hill in Italy
on the way to Assisi, surrounded by sunflower fields,

the sun and their faces as golden as the cross I bought
and the walls of the city thick on my tongue

when I tried to nail down all the things I never could say to him.
When I walked down the hill to the train, the sun

was cloistered to the west, and all the blooms turned away from me.
They may have been smiling, or they may have wept their seeds

for birds, or maybe those flowers know nothing of themselves
and just fold like origami in the gentle and tame hands of night.

THE WALLS

When I worked in a Mexican restaurant alongside the wall in Berlin, there were no Mexicans. The owners were from Texas and the employees from all over Europe, mostly Spain. I sifted through the beans for stones, peeled avocados, chopped onions, and after work fed the owners' parrot pistachios. I rode my bike alongside the wall to bars and gazed at the graffiti. My favorite was an image of an angel emerging from a blue shell.

Once my friend Elsie and I crossed the border to East Germany's gray streets. The buildings were covered in soot, and a lone playground on concrete had a swing structure, rusty, no children. Elsie said, *I wouldn't even want my father to live here, and I hate my father.* I turned to her and took her hand. On the way back, we stopped at a metro station. A drunk, skinny woman drank schnaps on a green bench. *Get out, you pigs,* she said.

Now I live in another country with a wall. The skies in this desert are as blue as that shell, but the angel left long ago. I do not know where she went.

THIRST

My dog barked in November
and trains came crashing through my forest
toward the lake where I walked
on waves of ice to deep water,
dove into its depth and swam to Chicago.
Kika the daredevil, they said,
I dumbfounded, staggered and stupefied
by my thirst to swim,
while railcars carried oil,
sleeping immigrants,
and black coal
the color of my spreading pupils
in the black-pepper night
where a blinking lighthouse
brought me home.

I left three times,
itinerant as a bird:
once to gallivant across the Alps
           to see my mother's hips in their stone,
once vagrant and roving through cities
           of asphalt to see my ambition grow,
once on a junket to Spain,
           where I picked oranges and drank wine.

I learned three languages
and collected dogs,
their paws against my leg,
my hands stroking fur as soft as dust.
I learned to hunt grouse with them in the forest,
where pines taught me about ascent,

the way they rise and swell
from their sappy trunks.
I learned to dance
on the edge of my nightmares
and in the summer I picked raspberries
for my children,
who slipped and spilled out of me,
out of the love
for the man,
gritty as soil.

In December I scraped ice
from my car's windows
so I could see where I was going.

My thirst was a mother with nowhere to go
but in and through a body,
tunneling like blood through
the winter's ground as patient
as the tulip bulbs it held.

BETWEEN YOU AND ME

Between you and me
lie snow-covered alleys
with footprints of cats
and frozen dust.
I walked those alleys as a child,
peeked into backyards
and a house where an old woman
cooked on her stove.

Between you and me
is always a child,
and you comb her hair,
and she wears a yellow dress
and hangs a blue bulb
on our Christmas tree.

I have traversed the alley
between you and me,
stomped my feet in the snow,
wondering where the old woman's
children went, wondering how
I can find you to tell you
about the child,
how you can't let her go.

Between you and me
lie ice and the ache of labor.
After our daughter was born,
you caught my blood and threw
it across the plains, and from it
rose yucca, its flowers as white

as the hospital walls that lay
between you and me
until I stopped bleeding.
And I did.

Now the cats are always hunting
and the snow is too frozen
for you to build the dragon
you always sculpted for us.
Branches lie etched in the white sky,
and we sit in the hot tub,
daughter dunking head in warm water,
and you say, *Look,*
look how they're always reaching,
and I look up at the web of branches
and how they finger the clouds
and I wonder what the old woman
was cooking, and I wonder
if she's still alive,
and I see that what lies
between you and me
has frozen roots
and its branches are the children
that rise over snow-covered alleys
that lie between you and me.

YELLOW

The aspen are turning early this autumn, their leaves
the color of the blouse you wore the day you died,

the day you wheezed and fought for air like those trees
that now exhale too soon because of our hot, dry earth.

That blond urchin still shoots me with water guns,
my daughter runs with dragonflies in the mountains,

and they keep wormless grass green as long as they can, sucking
up the Colorado River like a famished baby nursing.

Two years ago you died. I was writing on the sky
with a black pen, a hound coughed up the moon,

spider homes webbed our four corners,
and my son drew a crow, slashed shadow wings flying.

You died without me,
so I visited your body in the funeral home

and I took the white of your face and painted clouds,
those promising curves of rain the aspen craved

this summer before they began to die for the white
of snow. I know too much of death and little of life,

and the bears sniff dying light and den,
raspberries we didn't eat shrivel, and I bring

out the leather boots with the silver buckles that coax
my feet to the ground. I don't know what

you would think of me now, with my feathered round way
and the digging when it's too late to plant,

with my blue marriage and children who climb
and carry nails because our house always falls.

Now the apples are ripe, yellow dots the mountains,
and when I dream of you, you're young, wavy

brown hair, deep eyes always circled with war,
a paint brush in your hand. Paint me, Mother,

find me in the basement rummaging through everything I thought
I'd never find—the garnets, the portrait of father with the sunflowers,

the old picture of your mother wearing a dirndl. Roots
survive even when the petals we show the world shrivel.

Paint me, Mother,
paint me yellow.

www.ingramcontent.com/pod-product-compliance
Lightning Source LLC
Chambersburg PA
CBHW021020090426
42738CB00007B/844